FESTIVALS AND FOOD
India

Mike Hirst

WAYLAND

ies and book editor: Polly Goodman
Designer: Tim Mayer
Cover design: Wayland
cture researcher: Shelley Noronha

shed in 1998 by Wayland Publishers Ltd.
ted edition published in 2006 by Hodder Wayland, an imprint of
Hachette Children's Books
Wayland, an imprint of Hachette Children's Books
© Copyright 2006 Wayland

The website addresses (URLs) included in this book were valid at the time of going to press. However, because of the nature of the Internet, it is possible that some addresses may have changed, or sites may have closed down since publication. While the author and publishers regret any inconvenience this may cause the readers, no responsibility for any such changes can be accepted by either the author or the publisher.

British Library Cataloguing in Publication Data
Hirst, Mike, 1964-
India. – 2nd ed. – (Festivals and food)
1. Cookery, India – Juvenile literature 2. Festivals – India –
Juvenile literature 3. Food habits – India – Juvenile literature
4. India – Social life and customs – Juvenile literature
I. Title II. Hirst, Mike, 1964-. Flavour of India
641.5'954

ISBN-13: 978-0-7502-4842-6

Cover photograph: A woman selling vegetables in the city of Calcutta, in eastern India.
Title page: A Hindu wedding ceremony in Bangalore, in southern India.
Contents page: Lamps and incense for a family shrine at the festival of Divali.

Photograph and artwork acknowledgements
Cephas 16; Chapel Studios 19, 20 (top), 22 (bottom), 24 (left), 26 (right); David Cumming 13 (right); Eye Ubiquitous title page, 5 (top right), 5 (middle left), 5 (middle right), 5 (bottom right), 7 (top), 9, 10, 11, 12, 17, 23 (top); Impact cover, 5 (top left); Pankaj Shah 5 (bottom left), 6; Bruce Coleman 7 (bottom); Getty Images 8, 13 (left), 28; Christine Osborne 23 (bottom); Peter Sanders 14, 18, 20 (bottom), 24 (right); TRIP 26 (left); Wayland Picture Library 3, 22 (top), 27. Fruit and vegetable artwork is by Tina Barber. Map artwork on page 4 is by Hardlines. Step-by-step recipe artwork is by Judy Stevens.

Printed and bound in China

Hachette Children's Books, an Hachette Livre UK Company
338 Euston Road, London NW1 3BH

CONTENTS

India and its Food

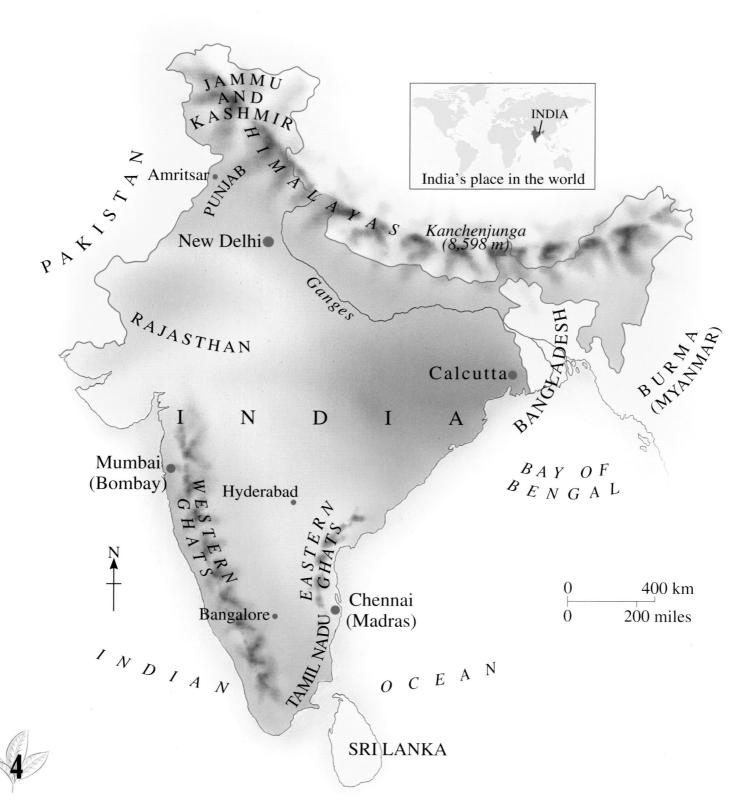

JAMMU
AND
KASHMIR

PAKISTAN

Amritsar

PUNJAB

HIMALAYAS

Kanchenjunga
(8,598 m)

INDIA

India's place in the world

New Delhi

Ganges

RAJASTHAN

BANGLADESH

Calcutta

BURMA
(MYANMAR)

I N D I A

Mumbai
(Bombay)

WESTERN GHATS

Hyderabad

EASTERN GHATS

BAY OF
BENGAL

N

Bangalore

TAMIL NADU

Chennai
(Madras)

0   400 km
0   200 miles

I N D I A N   O C E A N

SRI LANKA

FRUIT AND VEGETABLES

Vegetables are very important in India since millions of Indians are vegetarian.

RICE

India is the second-largest rice grower in the world. People eat rice with most meals in India, so it is a very important food.

SPICES

Indian food is famous for being spicy. People usually buy spices whole at markets. They crush them at home.

FISH

People who live near the coast in India, or beside rivers or lakes, eat lots of spicy fish dishes.

WHEAT

Most wheat in India is grown in the north. It is used to make many different types of Indian breads.

BEANS AND LENTILS

Beans and lentils are in many Indian dishes. They are very good for you because they contain protein.

Food and Farming

India is a vast country, which stretches from the snowy Himalayan mountains in the far north, to the sunny beaches of the Indian Ocean in the south.

India is famous for its many delicious recipes, and food is an important part of the Indian way of life. Even everyday dishes are carefully prepared. For religious festivals and other special occasions, Indian cooks spend days preparing a feast of food.

▼ Harvesting wheat in northern India, in the foothills of the Himalayas.

Rice and bread

Two foods are especially important in India: rice and bread. There are many different types of bread, such as *chapatis*, *purees,* or *nan* bread. Just about everyone eats some rice or bread every day.

Rice needs lots of sunshine and water to grow, so it is grown mainly in southern and eastern India, where there is the most rain. Bread is usually made from wheat. Most wheat is grown in the north of India, where there is not much rain for most of the year.

▲ Spreading out rice grains to dry in the hot sun of Tamil Nadu, southern India.

▼ In India, you find delicious cooked snacks for sale on almost every street corner.

Spices

Spices are an important part of Indian cooking. They come from a variety of different plants, and they all have strong flavours. Some spices, such as chillis, taste very 'hot'. If you eat a raw chilli, it makes a tingling, burning feeling on your tongue.

▼ British people having a picnic in India in 1911, when India was a British colony.

8

▲ Spices add colour as well as flavour to Indian foods.

The most common spices used in India are turmeric, ginger, garlic, coriander seeds or cloves. Most Indian spices need a hot climate to grow, so many are grown in the south-west. However, one spice, called saffron, comes from Kashmir in the far north. Saffron comes from the crocus flower. Indian cooks use it to give rice a delicate flavour.

Beans and Lentils

Other important foods in India are beans and lentils. There are several types of beans grown in India, such as red kidney beans, chickpeas, *moon dal* and *masoor dal*. They are all used to cook a kind of stew, called *dal*. Beans and lentils contain a lot of protein, which helps the body to grow and stay fit, so *dal* is very healthy. Flavoured with tasty spices, *dal* is delicious too!

▼ Beans and lentils for sale in Rajasthan, north-west India.

Regional Food

Each region of India has its own special dishes. People in Kashmir eat a special kind of *nan* bread, stuffed with fruit and nuts, called *Kashmiri nan*. Near the coast, people eat a lot of fish and seafood. In the port of Mumbai (Bombay), you might eat a dish called 'Bombay duck' – not a duck at all, but a small fish which local fishermen catch! In southern India, people love to eat soft, boiled rice cakes calles *idlis* and crispy pancakes called *dosas*.

▲ Fish from the Bay of Bengal, off India's eastern coast. Spicy fish dishes are popular in places near the sea, rivers or lakes.

A Hindu Wedding

About four out of every five Indians is a Hindu. They follow the religious teachings of Hinduism and worship the Hindu gods.

▼ Guests at a wedding feast in the countryside, eating from palm leaves.

Marriage is one of the most important events in a Hindu person's life. When a Hindu couple get married, all their friends and family gather to celebrate. In the countryside, the whole village often comes to the wedding.

Feast!

Wherever the wedding takes place, it is always followed by a huge feast, with enough food for hundreds or even thousands of people. The party, with singing, dancing and eating, can last as long as three days!

Many Hindus are vegetarians, which means they do not eat meat. At a Hindu wedding feast, there may not be any meat dishes at all. But there is sure to be a huge choice of spicy vegetable dishes.

▲ Cows are specially sacred animals to Hindus, so Hindus never eat beef.

◀ Food for a feast, including rice, poppadoms and a selection of spicy dishes.

▲ Spicy cauliflower and potatoes.

Vegetable dishes are named after the Hindi words for the vegetables they contain. *Gobi masaledar* means 'spicy cauliflower' in Hindi. *Gobi* means 'cauliflower' and *masaledar* means 'spicy'. There's a recipe for *gobi masaledar* on the opposite page.

To go with your vegetables at a wedding, you would also eat rice and breads, *dal*, pickles, and tasty side dishes called chutneys.

Gobi Masaledar

EQUIPMENT

Food processor
Knife
Deep saucepan
Wooden spoon

INGREDIENTS

1 Large cauliflower, broken into small pieces
1 Onion, 4 cloves garlic and 5 cm ginger, peeled and chopped
8 Tablespoons vegetable oil
1/2 Teaspoon turmeric
1 Large tomato, chopped

Fresh coriander leaves, chopped
1 Small green chilli, chopped
2 Teaspoons ground coriander
1 Teaspoon ground cumin
1 Teaspoon garam masala
2 Teaspoons salt
Juice of 1/2 a small lemon

Put the garlic, ginger and onion into the processor with 4 tablespoons of water. Blend into a paste.

Ask an adult to heat the oil gently in the saucepan and pour in the paste. Add the turmeric and fry for about 5 minutes.

Add the chopped tomato, coriander leaves and chilli, and fry for another 2 minutes.

Add all the other ingredients and 100 ml water. Cook on a low heat for 30–40 minutes, stirring every 10 minutes.

Always be careful with frying. Ask an adult to help you.

The wedding ceremony

For the wedding ceremony, the bride wears a bright-red *sari* with gold thread. Her hands are decorated with patterns of henna dye. She sits under a canopy, opposite the bridegroom, and in front of a sacred fire. A priest puts a cord around the couple's shoulders to join them together. Then the bride and bridegroom walk around the fire seven times, to show that they will go through the rest of their lives together.

▼ Painting traditional patterns on the bride's hands using henna.

A wedding ceremony ▶ in the city of Bangalore.

CONFETTI

At the end of the wedding ceremony, guests throw rose petals and rice over the couple for good luck. Rice is a symbol for a new life, and shows that everyone hopes the couple will have children. The tradition of throwing confetti at a wedding comes from this custom.

Ramadan and Id-ul-Fitr

Besides the Hindu religion, India also has a very large Muslim community. There are about 100 million Muslim people in India.

Ramadan is an important religious festival for India's Muslims. It is a time of fasting, which lasts for a month. During Ramadan, Muslims do not eat or drink anything during the hours of daylight. This is written in the Muslim holy book, the *Qur'an*. It reminds Muslims that all their food comes from their god, Allah.

▼ Before entering a mosque to pray, Muslims take off their shoes and wash to show their respect.

Breaking the Fast

Each evening when the sun sets, Muslim families get together for a meal. They are thankful that they have kept the fast for another day.

At the end of Ramadan, Muslims have the holiday of Id-ul-Fitr. They exchange presents and visit friends and relations. Since the fasting is over, they also enjoy a special Id-ul-Fitr meal.

HALAL MEAT

Muslims should only eat meat where the animal has been killed in a special way, which is set out in the Muslim law books. Meat prepared in this way is called 'halal' meat.

▼ The men of a Muslim family break the day's fast during Ramadan.

Id-ul-Fitr

The Id-ul-Fitr meal often begins with a light dish of sweet dates. For the main course, there is usually some meat. Muslims never eat pork or bacon because they believe that meat from pigs is unclean. However, many Muslims like to eat chicken or lamb, and kebabs are a Muslim speciality.

One of the most famous Muslim recipes, from northern India, is tandoori chicken. The chicken is smeared with a spicy red paste, and then baked in a clay oven, called a *tandoor*.

RAITA

Raita is a simple side dish made with yoghurt. It is delicious eaten with spicy kebabs or tandoori chicken. If the hot spices are burning your tongue, a mouthful of raita cools it down again. *Raita* is always best to eat when it is chilled. There is a recipe for *raita* on the opposite page.

Making sweets ▶ for Id-ul-Fitr.

Raita

EQUIPMENT

Colander   Chopping board
Vegetable peeler   Knife
Saucepan   Wooden spoon

INGREDIENTS

500g Yoghurt
2 Medium-sized new potatoes
$1/2$ Cucumber
1 Teaspoon caraway seeds
1 Teaspoon garam masala
Pinch of salt

1 Peel the potatoes and chop them into cubes.

2 Boil them in a saucepan of water for about 10 minutes, until they are just soft. Ask an adult to drain them and leave them to cool.

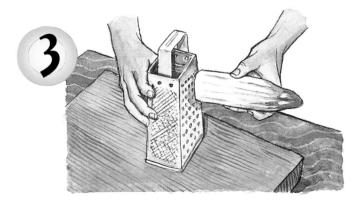

3 Peel the cucumber, then grate it, using the larger holes in the grater.

4 Mix the potatoes, cucumber and other ingredients into the yoghurt. Put the mixture in the fridge for a couple of hours before serving.

Always be careful with knives. Ask an adult to help you.

Guru Nanak's Birthday

The Sikh religion comes from the northern parts of India and Pakistan. The first Sikh teacher was Guru Nanak, who was born in 1469. He was friendly towards both Muslims and Hindus. In his teachings, Guru Nanak tried to join ideas from both the Muslim and Hindu religions.

▲ This painting shows Guru Nanak, with two sons and two followers.

A Sikh woman ▶ reading from the *Guru Granth Sahib*, the Sikh holy book.

Today there are Sikh communities in northern India, in all India's big cities and in many other places around the world.

Reading at the temple

Every November, Sikhs celebrate Guru Nanak's birthday. Each community gathers at its local temple, called a *gurdwara*. For the two days and nights leading up to the guru's birthday, men and women from the community take turns to read all the way through the Sikh holy book, the *Guru Granth Sahib*.

Everyone who hears the book being read eats a small portion of a sweet called *karah parshad*. *Parshad* means 'blessing'.

▲ Sikh men wear a turban as a sign of their religion.

Girls hold out ▶ their hands to receive *karah parshad*.

Cooking in the temple

▼ Sikhs eating in the Golden Temple, in Amritsar.

Every Sikh temple has its own kitchen, called a *langar*. This is where the *karah parshad* is prepared.

Sikhs believe that no member of the community should ever be allowed to go hungry. So besides *parshad*, the cooks in the *langar* prepare other food for people who come to the temple. This is usually bread, *dal* and vegetables.

At the most famous of all Sikh temples, the Golden Temple in Amritsar, many thousands of people are fed on Guru Nanak's birthday. Several servings are needed for everyone to eat.

BARFI

Barfi is a simple sweet. Like *karah parshad*, it is used by both Sikhs and Hindus as a blessing. Worshippers often receive a small piece of *barfi* when they visit a temple. There is a recipe for *barfi* on the opposite page.

Barfi

EQUIPMENT

Shallow dish or tin, lined with
   greaseproof paper

Knife

INGREDIENTS

125 g Full-cream
   powdered milk

250 g Castor sugar

5 Cardamom pods, crushed

12 Pistachio nuts, shelled
   and chopped

Margarine

1 Put the sugar and 125 ml water in a deep pan. Boil the water and then allow to simmer for 6–7 minutes, until the mixture turns into a gooey syrup.

2 Add the powdered milk, crushed cardamoms and pistachio nuts, and mix well.

3 Rub margarine over the greaseproof paper in the dish and pour in the mixture. Leave to cool.

4 When the *barfi* has set, cut it into squares or diamond-shaped pieces.

Always be careful with hot liquid. Ask an adult to help you.

Divali

Around the same time as Guru Nanak's Birthday, Hindus celebrate Divali, the Festival of Light.

At Divali, Hindus remember the story of one of their most popular gods, King Rama. Rama was born as a wealthy prince, but was forced to leave home by his wicked relatives. For many years he lived in the forest. Then his beautiful wife, Sita, was kidnapped by a demon called Ravana.

▼ This actor is playing the part of Hanuman, the monkey god, in a play of the Rama story.

This Divali poster ▶ shows Sarasvati, the goddess of knowledge (left), Lakshmi, the goddess of wealth (centre) and Ganesh, the elephant god who brings good luck.

26

Lamps and candles

Rama bravely set out to rescue Sita. Helped by Hanuman, the monkey god, Rama finally killed the demon and returned to his home city. There the people made him king.

At Divali, Hindus celebrate Rama's return home. They light tiny oil lamps and candles to show him the way home. Temples are ablaze with flickering lamps, and everyone lights up their doorways, windows and balconies.

Lamps and incense ▶ for Divali.

Sweets and snacks at Divali

▼ Cooking *jalebis*, a sweet snack, in Rajasthan.

Divali is a time for parties, and to visit friends and relatives. It is a tradition to take a gift of sweets to anyone you visit.

There are many kinds of rich, sticky sweets to choose from. *Jalebis* are swirls of sugary batter, fried in oil. *Gulab jamuns* are sweet dumplings in a gooey syrup.

SNACK STALLS

At Divali, roadsides in India are packed with snack stalls. They sell sweets, tasty savoury snacks, or milky drinks. *Lassi* is a popular drink made out of yoghurt, flavoured with sugar, salt, or different fruits. There's a recipe for banana *lassi* on the opposite page.

Banana *Lassi*

INGREDIENTS
500g Yoghurt
250 ml Iced water
4 Ripe bananas
2 Dessertspoons sugar

EQUIPMENT
Measuring jug   **Electric blender**
Knife

1

Measure out exactly 250 ml of iced water.

2

Peel and slice the bananas.

3

Put the yoghurt, water, bananas and sugar (if you want it) in an electric blender and mix until they are a smooth, thick liquid.

4

Serve in tall glasses.

Take care with the knife and electric blender. Ask an adult to help you.

Glossary

Chapatis   Round, flat Indian breads. *Chapatis* are flat because they are made without yeast, so they do not rise when they are cooked.

Chutney   A mixture of fruits or vegetables, spices and sugar, which is served as a side dish.

Confetti   Small pieces of coloured paper thrown at the bride and groom at weddings.

Fasting   Giving up eating and drinking.

Henna dye   Brown powder from the henna plant, which is made into a paste and used to decorate a bride's hands and feet.

Hinduism   The main religion practised in India. Hindus believe there is one God, but that God has many forms. A Hindu chooses one or more of these forms to worship.

Kebabs   Small pieces of meat or vegetable cooked on a skewer.

Muslim   A follower of Islam. Muslims believe in one God, Allah, and try to live their lives by doing exactly what Allah wants them to do.

Nan bread   A type of bread which has a little yeast added to it to make it rise slightly.

Purees   Small, puffy breads, which are deep-fried in a pan of hot oil.

Sari   A long piece of cloth, wrapped around the body and over one shoulder, which is the traditional dress of Indian women.

Sikhism   An Indian religion, which was begun in the sixteenth century by Guru Nanak.

Vegetarians   People who choose not to eat meat.

Topic Web and Resources

MATHS

Using and understanding data and measures (recipes).

Using and understanding fractions.

Using and reading measuring instruments: scales.

SCIENCE

Food and nutrition.

Plants in different habitats.

Separating mixtures of materials: sieving and dissolving.

Changing materials through heat.

GEOGRAPHY

Locality study.

Weather.

Farming.

Comparing physical landscapes.

Influence of landscape on human activities: farming and food festivals.

How land is used.

HISTORY

Trace the history of modern British food.

Investigate the different farming methods used over the past century

Festivals & Food TOPIC WEB

DESIGN AND TECHNOLOGY

Design and make a cereal box.

Design a poster to advertise a food product.

Technology used in food production.

Packaging.

MODERN FOREIGN LANGUAGES

Language skills.

Everyday activities: food.

People, places and customs.

ENGLISH

Make up a slogan to sell a food product.

Write a poem or story using food as the subject.

Write a list of food words and non-food words.

Write a menu you might find in an Indian restaurant.

BOOKS TO READ

A World of Recipes: India
by Julie McCulloch (Heinemann Library, 2002)

Country Insights: India
by David Cumming (Hodder Wayland, 2006)

Discover Other Cultures: Festivals Around The World
by Meryl Doney (Franklin Watts Ltd, 2002)

Facts About Countries: India
by Lizann Flatt (Franklin Watts, 2005)

Living In: India
by Ruth Thomson (Franklin Watts, 2002)

USEFUL WEBSITES

http://www.cia.gov/cia/publications/factbook/geos/in.html
The world factbook on India, with information on its geography, people, government and transportation.

http://www.webonautics.com/ethnicindia/festivals/
A bright and colourful website looking at the many different Indian festivals.

Index

Page numbers in **bold** mean there is a photograph on the page.